Principal Professional Development

CORWIN CONNECTED EDUCATORS SERIES

Content Curation: How to Avoid Information Overload
By Steven W. Anderson @web20classroom

5 Skills for the Global Learner: What Everyone Needs to Navigate the Digital World
By Mark Barnes @markbarnes19

Teaching the iStudent: A Quick Guide to Using Mobile Devices and Social Media in the K–12 Classroom
By Mark Barnes @markbarnes19

Connected Leadership: It's Just a Click Away
By Spike Cook @DrSpikeCook

All Hands on Deck: Tools for Connecting Educators, Parents, and Communities
By Brad Currie @bradmcurrie

The Missing Voices in EdTech: Bringing Diversity Into EdTech
By Rafranz Davis @RafranzDavis

Flipping Leadership Doesn't Mean Reinventing the Wheel
By Peter M. DeWitt @PeterMDeWitt

The Edcamp Model: Powering Up Professional Learning
By the Edcamp Foundation @EdcampUSA

Worlds of Making: Best Practices for Establishing a Makerspace for Your School
By Laura Fleming @NMHS_lms

Leading Professional Learning: Tools to Connect and Empower Teachers
By Tom Murray @thomascmurray and Jeff Zoul @Jeff_Zoul

Empowered Schools, Empowered Students: Creating Connected and Invested Learners
By Pernille Ripp @pernilleripp

Blogging for Educators: Writing for Professional Learning
By Starr Sackstein @mssackstein

Principal Professional Development: Leading Learning in the Digital Age
By Joseph Sanfelippo @Joesanfelippofc and Tony Sinanis @TonySinanis

The Power of Branding: Telling Your School's Story
By Tony Sinanis @TonySinanis and Joseph Sanfelippo @Joesanfelippofc

The Relevant Educator: How Connectedness Empowers Learning
By Tom Whitby @tomwhitby and Steven W. Anderson @web20classroom

Principal Professional Development
Leading Learning in the Digital Age

Joseph Sanfelippo
Tony Sinanis

FOR INFORMATION:

Corwin

A SAGE Company

2455 Teller Road

Thousand Oaks, California 91320

(800) 233-9936

www.corwin.com

SAGE Publications Ltd.

1 Oliver's Yard

55 City Road

London EC1Y 1SP

United Kingdom

SAGE Publications India Pvt. Ltd.

B 1/I 1 Mohan Cooperative Industrial Area

Mathura Road, New Delhi 110 044

India

SAGE Publications Asia-Pacific Pte. Ltd.

3 Church Street

#10-04 Samsung Hub

Singapore 049483

Printed in the United States of America

A catalog record of this book is available from the Library of Congress.

ISBN 978-1-4833-7988-3

This book is printed on acid-free paper.

Executive Editor: Arnis Burvikovs

Associate Editor: Ariel Price

Editorial Assistant: Andrew Olson

Production Editor: Amy Schroller

Copy Editor: Jared Leighton

Typesetter: C&M Digitals (P) Ltd.

Proofreader: Penelope Sippel

Cover and Interior Designer: Janet Kiesel

Marketing Manager: Lisa Lysne

SUSTAINABLE FORESTRY INITIATIVE

Certified Chain of Custody

Promoting Sustainable Forestry

www.sfiprogram.org

SFI-01268

SFI label applies to text stock

15 16 17 18 19 10 9 8 7 6 5 4 3 2 1

Contents

Preface

Welcome to the Corwin Connected Educators Series.

Last year, Ariel Price, Arnis Burvikovs, and I assembled a great list of authors for the fall 2014 books in the Corwin Connected Educators Series. As leaders in their field of connected education, they all provided practical, short books that helped educators around the world find new ways to connect. The books in the spring 2015 season will be equally as beneficial for educators.

We have all seen momentous changes for educators. States debate the use of the Common Core State Standards, and teachers and leaders still question the use of technology, while some of their students have to disconnect and leave it at home because educators do not know how to control learning on devices. Many of the series authors worked in schools where they were sometimes the only ones trying to encourage use of technology tools at the same time their colleagues were trying to ban it. Through their personal or professional learning networks (PLNs), they were able to find others who were trying to push the envelope.

This spring, we have a list of authors who are known for pushing the envelope. Some are people who wrote books for the fall 2014 season, while others are brand new to the series. What they have in common is that they see a different type of school for students, and they write about ideas that all schools should be practicing now.

Rafranz Davis discusses *The Missing Voices in EdTech*. She looks at and discusses how we need to bring more diverse voices to the connected world because those voices will enrich how we learn and the way we think. Starr Sackstein, a teacher in New York City, writes about blogging for reflection in her book, *Blogging for Educators.* Twitter powerhouse Steven W. Anderson returns to the series to bring us *Content Curation,* as do the very engaging Joseph Sanfelippo and Tony Sinanis with their new book, *Principal Professional Development.* Mark Barnes rounds out the comeback authors with his book on *5 Skills for the Global Learner.* Thomas C. Murray and Jeffrey Zoul bring a very practical how-to for teachers and leaders in their book, *Leading Professional Learning,* and Makerspaces extraordinaire Laura Fleming brings her expertise with *Worlds of Making.*

I am insanely excited about this book series. As a former principal, I know time is in short supply, and teachers and leaders need something they can read today and put into practice tomorrow. That is the exciting piece about technology; it can help enhance your practices by providing you with new ideas and helping you connect with educators around the world.

The books can be read in any order, and each will provide information on the tools that will keep us current in the digital age. We also look forward to continuing the series with more books from experts on connectedness.

As Michael Fullan has been saying for many years, technology is not the right driver, good pedagogy is, and the books in this connected series focus on practices that will lead to good pedagogy in our digital age. To assist readers in their connected experience, we have created the Corwin Connected Educators companion website where readers can connect with the authors and find resources to help further their experience. The website can be found at www.corwin.com/connectededucators. It is our hope that we can meet you where you are in your digital journey and bring you up to the next level.

Peter M. DeWitt, EdD
@PeterMDeWitt

About the Authors

Joseph (Joe) Sanfelippo is currently in his fourth year as the superintendent of the Fall Creek School District in Fall Creek, Wisconsin. Joe holds a BA in elementary and early childhood education from St. Norbert College, an MS in educational psychology from the University of Wisconsin-Milwaukee, an MS in educational leadership, and a PhD in leadership, learning, and service from Cardinal Stritch University. Joe was an elementary teacher, school counselor, and elementary principal before taking on the superintendent role. He cohosts the BrandED Radio Show on the Bam Radio Network. Joe serves on the Wisconsin Educator Effectiveness Teachscape Team developed by the Department of Public Instruction. His research interests include organizational and systems change in schools, personalized professional growth for staff, and advancing the use of social media in school districts. Joe can be found online at his website at www.jsanfelippo.com and on Twitter at @joesanfelippofc. Go Crickets!

Tony Sinanis is in his seventh year as the Lead Learner of Cantiague Elementary School in Jericho, New York. Cantiague was named a 2012 National Blue Ribbon School, and Tony received the 2014 New York State Elementary Principal of the Year Award and the national 2013 Bammy Award for Elementary School Principal of the Year. Tony taught at the elementary level for eight years and graduated from New York University with a degree in early childhood and elementary education and then went on to receive his master's degree in educational technology and an advanced certificate in educational leadership and technology from the New York Institute of Technology. Tony is currently enrolled in a doctoral program at the University of Pennsylvania where he is studying the relationship between active participation on Twitter and the professional development of principals. Tony is active on Twitter (@TonySinanis), serves as the founder and comoderator of #NYedchat, and has presented his work with social media and school branding at both national and local conferences. Finally, Tony cohosts the BrandED radio show with Dr. Sanfelippo; the show has been rated as high as number five on iTunes.

Introduction

A tale from Tony . . .

As the sole administrator in an elementary school, my opportunities to collaborate and grow as an instructional leader are limited. Although I do work closely with our staff, families, and students on a daily basis, these interactions do not necessarily provide me with opportunities to dialogue about the challenges, goals, and successes that are specific to being a school principal. Furthermore, with my emphasis being on meeting the needs of others, my personal and professional growth and development are rarely at the forefront of my daily practice. As school principals, our roles as instructional leaders are different than any other position within the world of education. As Lytle (2010) stated, we, as school principals, are constantly addressing the needs of the organization, trying to understand the actions of others, and keeping everything on course while making hundreds of decisions throughout the day, even though we may not have enough time to process, reflect, or collaborate with someone to ensure we are making the "best" decision possible in that moment.

When considering the role of the school principal, it becomes clear that the position is no longer singular in focus. The school principal is expected to go way beyond the administrator who sits in the office all day pushing papers around. Among the many challenges facing principals today is maintaining the balance between addressing the administrative mandates while also meeting the demands of being transformative instructional leaders. The school principal went from being a program manager/administrator in the 1960s and '70s to today when principals are expected to be transformational leaders who bring about change within the entire school community by successfully addressing both instructional needs (*instructional leader*) and administrative expectations (*administrator*) (Hallinger, 1992). An effective transformational leader, according to Hallinger (2003), is one who possesses strong instructional leadership abilities and skills that can be shared with the entire community.

The expectation of being an effective transformational instructional leader, along with the need to seek out current and relevant professional development opportunities, has led me in a new direction: to Twitter and the thousands of other educators using that platform to connect, share, learn, and grow. A socially networked online community, Twitter is one of the most popular social networking sites and is considered a form of microblogging that encourages educators to tweet and share their thoughts, opinions, and resources in 140 characters or less (Perez, 2012). As an educator, I have experienced the power of Twitter firsthand over the last two years, and this has led me to find out how principals may address their professional development needs by participating in this socially networked community. Twitter, like other social networking sites, functions as a social learning resource and space where educators can be exposed to a whole other type of discourse and literacy practice (Greenhow, 2009). Jane Hart, a social media and learning consultant, has classified Twitter as a tool for personal and informal learning that goes beyond the confines of any building (Galagan, 2009). Learners can use Twitter to ask and answer each other's questions, and Twitter can, in turn, help support collaboration and deeper understanding (Galagan, 2009). Since information on educators using Twitter for learning and professional development is limited because it is relatively uncharted territory, we will be offering a guide about what systems need to be put in place to begin supporting the professional development of principals using platforms such as Twitter.

Although one of our focal points will be Twitter, the bottom line is that we want to show that people—in this case specifically, principals—can learn through social interactions. Two of the newer platforms educators are using to connect, which we will discuss later in the book, are Voxer and Google Hangouts (GHO). These platforms function similarly to Twitter in that they allow educators to connect and share resources, ideas, and approaches that can impact practice almost immediately. The benefit to resources such as Voxer and GHO is that they allow for a verbal exchange of ideas, which is not an option on Twitter. When there can be discussion and people can see each other, which happens when using GHO, the experience is taken to another level because you can better understand things like tone and intent, which can be misunderstood when we are dealing just with text-based resources such as Twitter.

CHAPTER

1

The Expectations for Today's Principals

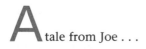

A tale from Joe . . .

I was a counselor and golf coach on the east side of Wisconsin. I had a great job, wonderful people to work with, and a comfortable lifestyle. When I decided to get my administration degree, I didn't really know when and if it would be used. I knew I loved to lead, but I was getting that need met in my current school. Coaching golf in high school was also an incredible job. As I finished the degree, I only applied for one job, and that was to help get my wife back into an area of the state that she really enjoyed. I was offered the job, and at the last golf match of the year, I was telling the other coaches in the conference that I was

(Continued)

(Continued)

leaving to be a principal. Their support for the move was . . . nonexistent! "Are you out of your mind?" "How old are you . . . thirty?" And my favorite, "Are you really giving up the golf job to get yelled at by parents and teachers?!?" Clearly, they were not on board with the move. I think part of my thought process was that it could be different. I also figured I had spent enough time in that office as a kid, so I knew how things operated! People usually get into administration because they have worked for a wonderful administrator and want to emulate him or her, or they have worked for a horrible administrator and know they can do it better. I had the opportunity to be in both scenarios. The idea that we could make this job whatever we wanted was really enticing to me. The principalship does not have to be what it was when we were kids. If we are given the opportunity, it can be and has been one of the best jobs I have ever had.

When considering the role of the principal, many envision the disciplinarian who handles all the behavior problems, the organizer of all things unfolding throughout the school day, or the individual who supervises the main office. Although these are responsibilities that typically fall under the purview of the principal, the daily expectations go way beyond these needs. A school leader today is supposed to act as an entrepreneur and a person of vision, able to inspire, empower, and motivate his staff under the auspices of a shared mission statement that fosters common goals for the entire community (Engels, Hotton, Devos, Bouckenooghe, & Aelterman, 2008). The position of principal has evolved tremendously over the last century from a basic program manager or administrator to today's expectation that a principal is a transformational leader who shapes instruction and impacts student performance (Hallinger, 1992). Transformational approaches to leadership expect that the principal is able to communicate a vision for the school that becomes a common goal for the entire community (Leithwood & Jantzi, 2000) and to ensure that sound instructional practices are permeating the classrooms, which lead to high levels of student achievement. This is what the school principal is expected to do today—be a transformational instructional leader and still oversee the daily administrative responsibilities of the building.

Hallinger (2003) conceptualizes instructional leadership in the following three dimensions: defining the school's mission, managing the instructional program, and promoting a positive school learning climate. When analyzing the expectations of being an instructional leader, school principals must carefully consider the learning unfolding within their schools. James Lytle (2010) wrote about his experiences as a principal in Philadelphia. He described how he discovered leading for learning, as opposed to just leading, while serving as the principal of Parkway School. In that school, Lytle spent time developing a clear understanding of the strengths and needs of the entire school community. He also devoted time to encouraging innovation and risk-taking on the part of the staff and students. Additionally, Lytle spent a lot of his time supporting the staff in their work and promoting the concept of entrepreneurship among the teachers. This was a way to help develop human, social, and organizational capital as a means to his desired end, which was to improve the learning opportunities for students. Although Lytle describes the work specific to one school, from our personal experiences as school principals over the last decade, his efforts reflect what we view as the general expectations for a transformational instructional leader in our schools today.

EXPECTATIONS OF TRANSFORMATIONAL INSTRUCTIONAL LEADERS (AKA BUILDING PRINCIPALS)

- Lead for learning—be the lead learner
- Have a clear understanding of the strengths and needs of the entire school community
- Be visible—be in classrooms and learning spaces throughout the day

- Support staff in their efforts to be innovative risk-takers with their learning and teaching
- Focus on student learning
- Communicate a vision for the school that is embraced by all constituent groups
- Ensure that sound (research-based) instructional practices are the norm in each classroom
- Offer the supports and resources necessary for high levels of student achievement
- Inspire, motivate, and empower all members of the learning community
- Be transparent and focus on telling the school story

There is widespread research that speaks to the specific impact of principal leadership on student performance (Supovitz, Sirinides, & May, 2010; Waters, Marzano, & McNulty, 2003), which is very much a part of being a transformational leader. A recent study indicated that the learning-centered leadership of the principal, which emphasizes instruction and student performance, enhances the prediction of student outcomes on standardized assessments beyond the prediction based on students' socioeconomic statuses alone. Principals who devoted a significant portion of their time to instructional leadership found that this eclipsed their focus on other "managerial" aspects of their job as the effects on students and their performance was evident (Reardon, 2011).

Boyatzis and McKee (2005) also wrote extensively about the resonant leader who could impact change within the organization by building resonant relationships with those around him or her. Transformational leaders and resonant leaders are one and the same because they can impact sustainable change within a learning community in a balanced and effective way. Boyatzis and McKee argue that resonant leaders inspire their organizations and communities to reach for goals that seemed unattainable in the past. In order to achieve this level of resonant leadership, which we would argue is the goal of many building principals, Boyatzis and McKee state that great leaders are emotionally intelligent and are mindful of the needs of those around them. Furthermore, they believe that great leaders are able to inspire the community through an optimistic perspective and a clear vision focused on collective goals. In light of these characteristics described by Boyatzis and McKee, there seems to be a direct correlation between the idea of resonant leaders and the expectation that current building principals are transformational instructional leaders who are able to face challenges and difficulties by focusing on a common vision intended to impact the community in a positive way. In considering the layered impact that a principal's instructional leadership can have on variables such as daily instruction, student performance, and the functionality of the educational community as a whole, an examination of the professional development opportunities that currently exist for principals must be undertaken.

Effective principals (a broad category with many characteristics, depending on who is surveyed) can manage the organization as a whole and the implementation of curriculum as long as they have the appropriate professional support and development (Elmore & Burney, 1999). Principals must deal with competing expectations and with the dilemmas inherent in concurrently overseeing the building, supervising instruction, being available to members of all constituent groups, delegating, accepting responsibility, and leading professional development and learning opportunities for the entire staff (classroom teachers, aides, specialists, etc.). Multiple personal and professional qualities seem to be needed to carry out the job successfully. As a result of these daily expectations (or pressures, depending on one's position), principals have felt a need for professional development to help them perform their arduous and ambiguous role successfully (Johnson, 1994). This is inherently one of the biggest problems facing the implementation of successful professional development for effective principals. If the educational community cannot agree on the job description of the effective principal and, in turn, the skills necessary to be effective in the position, how can "necessary" professional development opportunities become available? A distinct answer is lacking here, but there is clearly a need for professional development that can be tailored and personalized to support effective principals and their daily work.

CHAPTER 1—TWO TAKEAWAYS AND A TIP

- Takeaway #1—A school leader/building principal today is supposed to act as an entrepreneur (an innovator and disrupter) and a person of vision, be able to inspire the community, empower those around him or her, and motivate her or his staff under the auspices of a shared vision statement that fosters common goals for the entire community. The principal must be able to be the voice for what the community believes in and stands for.

- Takeaway #2—In considering the layered impact that a principal's instructional leadership can have on variables such as daily instruction, student performance, and the functionality of the educational community as a whole, an examination of the professional development opportunities that currently exist for principals must be undertaken.

- Tip—There will never be extra time in your day. Lead learners model learning by integrating the learning into an already full day. Begin by developing the learning in places you already go on a regular basis. Setting Google Alerts on a particular topic, developing a Twitter list of educational organizations or leaders, or creating a list of podcasts will help you to create consistency in your learning.

CHAPTER
2

The Importance of Professional and Personal Development

As a principal in a suburban school district in western Wisconsin, Curt Rees has always believed in the power of professional development. He believes that if we do not take charge of our own learning, someone else will. If we are told to go to something, it often doesn't fit our personal need when it comes to professional growth. The more we can take control of our learning, the more investment we have in the process. The impact of social media on that professional development has been profound. Getting a chance to connect with like-minded principals across the world went from an interest to a lifestyle for Curt.

Curt started using Twitter in 2009, and it has turned into one of his first stops when it comes to personal professional development.

He feels it is essential that you model for your staff and your students. The needs of our kids keep changing; the expectations from the district, state, and national levels are consistently changing. We need to model the idea that with constant change, we need to be continuous learners. In doing this, we need to build learning into our daily routines. He believes modeling continuous learning through reading is extremely important. Not only do we need to be modeling the learning process, we need to be intentional about sharing and how it might apply to people in our organizations. He adds a piece to his weekly update to his staff entitled "Brain Food." This has been a fantastic resource to pass along for people to look at on their own time. In addition, through conversations with staff members, you can address specific needs that match your knowledge. He encourages people to build time into their daily routine. . . . There will never be more time in the day. His advice is to find something you have an interest in, passion for, or feel knowledgeable about and begin from that place. Sometimes the logistics of sharing are made easier if the topic is an area of interest. As learners, we are more likely to invest in the process if we have a distinct interest in what we seek out for professional development. Start with a topic that you enjoy, and begin a routine from there.

High-quality professional development is critical to the process of improving the quality of teaching, learning, and leadership in our school systems (Caldwell, 1986). Fullan (2009) shared that, although there is an expectation that school leaders are instructional leaders, most principals don't know what instructional leadership looks like and how to do it. Research has indicated that principals are extremely interested in receiving professional development to improve their leadership skills and abilities within the school context (Spanneut, Tobin, & Ayers, 2012). The continuous professional development of principals has been recognized as being essential for strengthening their "capacity to improve instruction [and] create a school culture of shared leadership, collaboration and high expectations for all students" (Spanneut et al., 2012).

While principals undoubtedly serve an important role through their position as instructional leaders in developing high-performing schools, the research on what knowledge, proficiencies, and aptitudes principals need to be successful within the school setting is still emerging and being explored. Without the establishment of a solid foundation, it has been a challenge for researchers to target what administrator professional development opportunities should focus on, what forms they should take, or how their successes should be evaluated (Grissom & Harrington, 2010).

As a result of these issues, the literature on professional development for principals is surprisingly underdeveloped. The lack of information about principal professional development leaves educators and policy makers with little guidance on approaches for strengthening and supporting current school leaders who have dedicated themselves to being transformative leaders who are expected to positively affect teaching and learning (Brown, Anfara, Hartman, Mahar, & Mills, 2002). Undeniably, while the National Staff Development Council reports that teacher professional development is provided at a three-to-one ratio compared to principal professional development (Caldwell, 1986), even a perfunctory glance at other literature and studies reveals that the difference in research attention paid to the two areas of professional development is many times larger, with principal professional development potentially being somewhat neglected. Fortunately, with the explosion of the digital age, we are starting to see things shift in regard to how school principals are accessing professional development opportunities. With the availability of webinars, online courses, and socially constructed networks, such as a personal learning network (PLN) through Twitter, Voxer, Google+ Communities, and Google Hangouts (GHOs), school principals can now access different types of professional development from anywhere and at any time.

The idea of school principals developing a PLN—a network of peers or mentors with whom they can learn, work, and grow—speaks to a professional development model that could be accessed more often as it is built on the pillars of social learning, which we know to be an effective way to learn. Gerard, Bowyer, and Linn (2008) suggested that principals prefer professional development activities that engage them in reviewing curricula and student work with other principals, which again reinforces the concept of principals being professionally developed in a collaborative fashion. This type of learning speaks to the practices currently unfolding on social media, especially in spaces such as Twitter and Google+ Communities. Educators are sharing links to resources, ideas, and best practices on a regular basis, and many school principals are engaged in these communities.

Boerema (2011), after interviewing eight new school leaders, found that these leaders felt they could meet with success when they were supported. Support came in the form of mentors listening, mentors expressing concern for their well-being, and mentors giving encouragement and affirming the work of the new leaders. The mentor supporting the new leader again speaks to the notion of learning through interaction and connects to the idea of the master supporting the apprentice. One common thread connecting these studies is that they all feature qualities of social learning theory, as the school principals were experiencing professional development through social interactions.

Social learning refers to personal experiences within a specific context and social aptitude (Wenger, 2000). Wenger argues that within a social learning system, which could apply to any context, learning is defined both socially and historically. Any knowledge developed is a result of displaying competencies defined in social communities, which in this case would be the PLN on varied social media platforms (Voxer, GHO, Twitter, or Google+ Communities). For example, if a new teacher is hired by a school, he or she is the newcomer who is trying to learn how the community works, and the new teacher relies on the competency of the experienced members around him or her to refine his or her skills and get acclimated to the community. On the other end of the spectrum, the veteran knows how the community works but may have a personal experience that she or he wants to share with the community to enhance the competencies of the entire group.

Learning within the PLN may also feature exchanges between a mentor and apprentice, such as what recently happened through the School Administrator Virtual Mentor Program (#SAVMP), which was facilitated by George Couros and Amber Teamann. In this type of connection, a relatively inexperienced school principal learned from, instead of with, a more experienced school principal. Lave and Wenger (1991) presented the idea of situated learning, which they detailed with examples about different apprenticeships where learning occurred in situated ways. In the apprentice model, the expert often served as a model/scaffold for the novice because this approach is rooted in the belief that a novice initially needs explicit support to perform tasks that will later be performed independently. Ondrejka (2008) takes it a step further in his study and builds on the idea of legitimate peripheral participation (LPP), initially suggested by Lave and Wenger (1991), where people learn best when they spend time with other people who have mastered the skills they wish to learn, much like an apprentice would work with a master. With that being said, Lave and Wenger argue that the novice's learning didn't only occur through interactions with the expert; instead, the novice also developed understandings based on interactions with the community as a whole. They qualify this type of learning—active engagement in social practice—as legitimate peripheral participation because participants have entry points to social connections that lead to learning experiences, such as what happens to members of a PLN.

Professional practitioners, in this case school principals, grow from actively engaging with clear content and other members of their organizations, or related professional groups, and from sustained opportunities to reflect on and apply new knowledge to their work settings. Meeting the challenge of improving instruction and student performance in many of our schools, especially those in urban and rural settings, will partially depend on school leaders who can effectively lead such improvement as a result of their strong skill sets. But developing principals who can lead teachers and students to a new level of performance is a daunting task, and as stated earlier, the opportunities for professional development and growth are not in abundance for principals (Brown et al., 2002). Barnes, Camburn, Sanders, and Sebastian (2010) conducted a study that focused on urban principals and district-level professional development (DPD). The DPD in the study aimed to reduce the time and intellect that principals in one urban district put into noninstructional matters (i.e., the managerial-type tasks). The program focused them instead on content, including best practice theory and research related more directly to improving the overall instructional practices of the teachers and academic achievement of the students. From their own findings, the DPD was the only program that helped principals with these tasks, and it did so through their active participation in the ongoing social-learning environment or community of practice that the program cultivated and expected. During interviews conducted in June 2005, the principals who participated in the DPD program reported that the team, or cohort, approach was a key benefit of their early DPD experience. In the end, although most principals who participated in the DPD did not radically change their daily work in regard to instructional leadership, their cohort experience within the DPD encouraged them to refine their current practices and enhance their daily work on varied levels. This study speaks to the idea that principals need professional development opportunities related to instruction, and when these opportunities are presented in a cohort model, much like what occurs through social or situated-learning experiences, there is a positive impact on the transference of learning within the group to practice within the school.

When considering that principals are often the only leaders in the schools and don't easily have access to cohorts, mentors, or coaches to support their development, developing a PLN using social media as the platform could be a way for principals to connect with like-minded people, such as what occurs in communities of practice, and personalize learning for the purposes of enhancing their own settings. As Wenger (1998) hypothesized, communities of practice are a vital part of our daily lives and exist almost everywhere, from our families to our work to our educational institutions. The idea of communities of practice directly links to social learning theory because individuals are learning by engaging in and contributing to the practices of their communities, and in turn, the communities of practice are learning by refining their practices and adding to their membership. The idea of a community of practice also connects to the types of professional development opportunities that include structures such as the cohort model, one in which individuals learn from coaches or mentors through social interactions and potentially develop communities of practice.

Although professional development opportunities for school principals are limited, we do have a better understanding of the structures that successful professional development experiences feature. These structures rely heavily on the notions suggested by social learning theory and communities of practice in that individuals learn effectively through interactions and connections with others. As digital learning opportunities continue to expand for school principals, we see many of these same successful structures in place, such as learning through social connections and interactions. For example, the idea of the PLN and the interactions that are at its core also connect to features present within the participatory culture that exists in our world today.

Although the role of social media (specifically resources such as Twitter, Voxer, and GHO) in education and its impact on the professional development of educators (specifically school principals) is relatively unexplored territory, we are starting to see studies emerge connecting the two ideas. Alderton, Brunsell, and Bariexca (2011) surveyed and analyzed the public Twitter feeds of ten classroom teachers to determine the reasons for which educators use Twitter. The classroom teachers were then given an eleven-item survey consisting of multiple-choice and open-ended questions to get information directly from the participants about how they use Twitter. All of the participants indicated that Twitter allowed them to establish and nurture connections with other educators beyond their immediate vicinity as a way to share resources, collaborate, engage in conversation, and provide or receive support whenever necessary, which is known as a personal or professional learning network (PLN).

In a study conducted by Elias (2012), he specifically analyzed the tweets of five educational leaders to capture how they were using Twitter. The study involved an analysis of tweets coupled with interviews of each participant. In the end, Elias found that more than half of the tweets he analyzed were practice-related and that several of the participants were using Twitter for regular social interactions, which often led to learning. Furthermore, upon interviewing the participants, they consistently communicated that they used Twitter for the purposes of professional development because it allowed them access to an abundance of resources. When probed to consider the platform, in this case Twitter, the participants consistently communicated that their learning came as a result of their connections, not just as a result of being on Twitter. In another recent dissertation study, Brennan (2013) interviewed thirteen school leaders to discover how they were using virtual learning as a form of professional and organizational growth. The message that was communicated consistently was that these school leaders were using Twitter as a forum to connect with other building leaders, and these connections were leading to their own growth and in some cases impacting the growth of their organizations.

These studies, which analyze Twitter as a platform, indicate that educators learn through social interactions and connections with others when they are members in a "low-barrier" setting with other like-minded educators looking to learn and enhance their craft. Being that social media platforms such as Voxer, GHO, and Google+ Communities are relatively new, there is limited research about their specific impact in the world of education. Fortunately, these varied social media platforms share important features, and thus, we would argue that the research focused on Twitter could be generalized in different ways to apply to the aforementioned social media platforms.

Taking this idea a step further, what we know about social learning theory is that people can learn well in a social context when they have opportunities to collaborate with mentors, coaches, cohorts, or networks that offer support and resources and are available for collaboration. With that in mind, social learning theory could serve as the foundation upon which some professional development opportunities for principals could be constructed to support their evolution and indirectly impact their learning organizations, students, and surrounding communities in positive ways. The planning of effective professional development opportunities for school principals must be cognizant of the evolving role of this position.

As the role and expectations of the principal continue to evolve and grow, the need for current, connected, relevant, and personalized professional development opportunities and collaboration with other educators and leaders is critical. The research spotlighted here speaks to the power of effective professional development for principals happening in a collaborative way through the cohort model (Cochran-Smith & Lytle, 2009), as opposed to it happening in isolation, such as when attending a workshop or conference or taking a graduate-level course (Fullan, 2009).

As we closely analyze the idea of professional development for school principals, we must start to consider the blurry line that separates it from one's personal development. Although we have traditionally thought of professional development as the only type of development a school principal needs, what we are starting to see is that principals evolve on a personal level when they connect with other educators and become active members of a personal learning network or professional learning community—a safe group where they can exchange ideas, discuss situations, and fluidly move from novice to expert. For example, a group of educational leaders may be participating in a Voxer group discussion about the book *The Miracle Morning* by Hal Elrod, and as a result, one school principal in the group may refine his or her personal practices in the morning in order to achieve the "miracle morning." In turn, this change in personal morning routines might directly, or indirectly, impact the leader's professional world, and hence, we begin to see the blurring of the lines between personal and professional development.

Another example of the idea of personal development overlapping with professional development comes to us from Lisa Meade, who is a middle school principal from New York State. She shares how becoming a connected educator helped amplify her voice . . .

The inner core (of my PLN) just keeps me going because they are like fuel. The outer core (of my PLN), they give me ideas or they say things and confirm what I agree with or sometimes don't agree with, and this is important because it forces me to think. This also impacts me as a blogger because when I put ideas out there and get feedback from people, sometimes people that I look up to and admire, that makes my voice stronger within my own building because it's been validated. In the beginning, when I was on Twitter, I really didn't have a voice. I was just this lady trying to figure it out and retweeting a lot of things, but I don't think I retweeted anything controversial because I hadn't defined my voice . . . yet.

CHAPTER 2—TWO TAKEAWAYS AND A TIP

- **Takeaway #1**—The brain likes to be social. We learn better together . . . Start to grow your learning network by reaching out to people online and in person. Find a person or people you connect with online, and find out whom they are connected to by looking at Twitter lists, Google+ connections, or LinkedIn connections.

- **Takeaway #2**—Being the lead learner means leading the learning. We need to find opportunities to grow even outside of professional development like conferences and workshops. Start your day with an article or podcast. Share that through a social network of choice.

- **Tip**—If you are an educational leader, you must take control of your own learning and personalize it in a way that makes the most sense for you . . . Nurture a PLN, create a cohort of local peers, or connect with a mentor; whatever the form, your professional development must be a high priority.

CHAPTER

3

The Power of
Social Media

As we know, the power of the personal or professional learning network (PLN) can help support the professional and personal development of school leaders. Tony shares with us his journey toward becoming a connected educator. . . .

It was late January and our family was preparing for our son's upcoming surgery (that's a whole other type of Isolation Island). Being that there was ample stress permeating our lives, both my wife and I took the opportunity to unwind with some reading each night after tucking the little guy in. I was finally catching up on some professional reading when I came across an issue of *Scholastic Administrator*. I was immediately intrigued by the cover that featured a man holding a phone in front of his face and the Twitter "mascot" sitting atop the phone (I know many of you know the image I'm describing.). I had heard a lot about Twitter but was extremely resistant to try it because I always associated it with celebrities (the Kanye Wests and Britney Spearses of the world) sharing random thoughts and details about their lives that I had no interest in reading. There was also some talk about Twitter in our district a couple of years ago in regard to communicating with parents, but once again, I was resistant, mainly because I didn't know much about the tool. But here was this guy, a fellow principal in New Jersey, on the cover of the magazine, spotlighting how he used Twitter to enhance his craft. Being that I am always looking for ways to make myself a better instructional leader, educator, and colleague, I dove into the article and soon found myself hooked and ready to create my own Twitter account!

The guy on the cover turned out to be Eric Sheninger (@NMHS_Principal), and he was using Twitter for the purposes of professional development and connecting with other like-minded educators. As the principal of an elementary school, with no other administrator in the building, the leadership experience often leaves me feeling like I'm on my own little island—Isolation Island to be exact. Don't get me wrong, there is rarely a minute when I am actually alone while at school, but the ability to dialogue, problem solve, or collaborate with other administrators doesn't occur on a regular basis (even though I work with many dedicated educators). There is something so exciting and inspiring that happens when dialoguing with other instructional leaders and administrators about their experiences, successes, failures, and passions. Although I have attended conferences in the past, the experiences didn't necessarily have a lasting impact on my professional development because the ability to brainstorm, expand, and collaborate with others on the next steps was still that missing link.

Well, I am happy to share that Twitter has changed all of that for me—BIG TIME! Since I joined Twitter almost three years ago, my whole professional world has been thrown on its head—and that's a great thing! I can honestly say that I have learned more about teaching, learning, and instructional leadership in the last few years than I had learned in the decade prior. Since joining Twitter and learning the ropes (I still have a lot to learn.), I feel like

I jumped off of Isolation Island and made my way to the Island of Instructional Leaders (and Pioneers)! So what have I learned since joining Twitter? How have I been impacted as a leader since joining Twitter? Here are just a few things that have happened for me since joining Twitter. . . .

1. I have developed an amazing PLN filled with other passionate and knowledgeable educators who challenge me to think and push myself to new levels and in directions I never imagined. My PLN is made up of other principals, educators, central office administrators, and lifelong learners. There are too many to name individually, but I am grateful to each of them because I have gained something from them that has made me a better leader and educator.

2. I get to follow some of the people in education who I respect and admire—Todd Whitaker, Heidi Hayes Jacobs, Alfie Kohn, Kathy Schrock, and Fountas & Pinnell, just to name a few. Not only do I get to read what they're thinking about or working on, but I can reach out to them directly with a question or comment and can usually get a response!

3. I have learned the power of the HASHTAG and how using the right tag unlocks a whole other world of professional conversations and sharing of ideas. Twitter chats have gained a great deal of momentum in the educational world. A Twitter chat is a scheduled online conversation organized by a moderator and filtered through a hashtag. A moderator or group of moderators will ask questions and end their tweets with a particular hashtag. Participants in the chat will answer the questions and add the hashtag. The result is an ongoing discussion, usually for sixty minutes, revolving around a specific subject in education. Whether it's the #ptchat on Wednesday evenings, which targets parents and teachers, the #NYedchat on Monday nights, which targets New York State educators, or the #edchat on Tuesdays, which gathers all educators around a general topic, there are literally hundreds of people online sharing ideas about a specific question, topic, or book, and the flow of ideas is incredible.

4. I have learned about Zite and Flipboard, which have literally changed the way I start my day. I cannot begin getting ready for the day if I don't spend time reading through the blogs, posts, and articles organized by Zite or Flipboard for me.

5. I have learned about Google Docs (and many other Google components), and it has shown me different ways to harness and focus the power of collaboration—what an amazing (and FREE) resource! In fact, if it weren't for Google Docs, Joe and I would not have been able to write our first book on the power of branding in education.

6. I have learned about Evernote, which has literally changed my professional life. It is an incredible app that allows me to type up stuff, take pictures, and more, and access the material from any device where I have downloaded the app because it syncs. So while doing walkthroughs each day in the building, I walk around with my iPad and take notes using Evernote. Then, when I get home at night, those notes are on my laptop, which makes my life so much easier when offering specific praise or feedback. I will definitely be using Evernote for my formal observations in the future!

7. I have learned about Diigo, which is such an amazing tool whose potential I haven't even fully realized yet. Basically, it allows me to visit different websites, read through them, make notes or highlight parts of the text, and then bookmark it to my Diigo account so I can access it later. And I can access Diigo from any computer, so all my bookmarks travel with me—AMAZING!

8. I was inspired to share the world of Twitter with our staff and colleagues through a voluntary training session that most of the staff attended! It was great to see fellow educators get inspired and avail themselves to this new medium for professional development and for becoming a connected educator! At this point, 85 percent of the learning spaces at #Cantiague are tweeting on a daily basis, and this tweeting is helping brand our space and tell our collective story.

9. I have learned about some great online resources, like Mentimeter, Yola, TodaysMeet, Twurdy, and Socrative, just to name a few. Check them out whenever you get a chance because

they can change the way you do things in your classrooms and in your school.

10. I started my own blog, which has given me voice that I never knew existed. I use Blogger for my postings, and I am loving every minute of blogging. I find Blogger to be user friendly and the steps for getting started and refining my blog straightforward and easy to follow. Blogging makes me feel empowered and has allowed me a whole other outlet for my ideas, successes, failures, and passions as they relate to the world of education.

These are just a few of the things I have learned over the last couple of years since joining Twitter and sharing my tweets with the world. Needless to say, I have taken my professional development into my own hands, and the experience has been liberating. Sometimes I feel like I am learning so much that I don't know where to begin, but I have come up with a system for that too. I Diigo the things I want to hold on to and access them when I am ready to learn something new. I can honestly say that not a day goes by where I don't learn something new ever since I made the move from Isolation Island to the Island of Instructional Leaders!

The stories about how principals are taking control of their professional development using various digital tools don't end with Tony. Lisa Meade, whom we met in the last chapter, shares the following reflections on the influence that being connected has had on her own personal and professional development through the presence of her PLN and those imperative social interactions and connections. . . .

There are people I follow on Twitter who inspire me, but then there are some people with whom I've been able to take it a step further. There are people who I really admire, and I hope to develop skills that I think they have that I want to have and use in my school. It is not just about reading tweets.

(Continued)

(Continued)

Meeting certain people face to face, attending their workshops, reading their blogs, or getting ideas from them verbally also helps me learn and grow. I actually think the PLN has different levels. There is an inner PLN circle, where I have strong personal connections, and then there is an outer PLN circle, where I just read what they put out and share with the world. The entire PLN has allowed me to broaden my school's reach and flatten the walls so I can connect with people from across the world who will make me better at the work I do in my school and district. That is the best professional development I have had in years!

Jimmy Casas, who is a high school principal in Iowa and was named the 2012 Iowa Secondary Principal of the Year, shared the following about the power of his PLN, which impacts his learning and interest in sharing with the world. . . .

Twitter has allowed me to make these connections, so it always goes back to relationships, and the relationships really are the fundamental core to everything that happens. It's the floor of connectivity that allows you to meet people, build these relationships, begins to expand to all these things that they just talk about, and then opens up doors that I never knew existed. Being connected on social media allowed me to continue to connect with others and learn from others but also provide resources back to others and build this community—expand our community beyond our school. That's one of the things I love about social media: everybody is willing to help everybody. I recognize that at any time if I need something, I can reach out to my network, and I know they'll help me. But I also think it's giving up yourself first. I think people recognize that, and I want to give back because you are willing to take time for people and to serve people and support people.

Daisy Dyer Duerr, a K–12 principal in Arkansas, shared the following reflection on the power of Twitter, in that it gives her access to a powerful PLN where she can learn, grow, and exchange ideas. . . .

I would say that Twitter is my go-to resource for professional development because I have a great professional and personal learning network. It gives me access to the people that I need to ask specific questions to so that I can learn and enhance my craft. For example, if I were to have a personnel issue or a personality issue with a staff member or community member, I would call Jimmy Casas. He's such a personal person, and although I'm really good with relationships, he's totally astronomical. I think that's something Twitter has really done for me: it's made me engage with the right people to do the right things, not only for my school but also to push myself to learn more. I think that's what is so engaging for me about Twitter. Everybody in the greater group there is easily accessible, and that is where the learning starts and happens. I think that just everybody being so excited about learning and everybody being so fired up about the idea of coming together and working together for a different good is what's really positive within the PLN and specifically Twitter, which is why it is my go-to for professional development.

Michael Berry, who is an elementary principal in Vermont, shares how Twitter has become his main source of professional development and, at the same time, held him accountable for being an effective leader. . . .

I essentially rely on social media for just about all my professional development. I think when I first started on Twitter, I wouldn't have called it professional development because the world didn't accept the idea, but now people are starting to accept it. Mind you, I rely on a couple of colleagues locally and then colleagues worldwide with social media. For a lot of research on a random day, whether I'm in a healthy debate with a colleague about the value of something or reflecting on the power of connecting with our families and in classrooms, I just throw a little thing out on Twitter, and within seconds, hundreds of other people send me everything that I needed.

(Continued)

(Continued)

As you know, being a principal is really isolating, and you can have a colleague five feet away, and you're still isolated. No one's going through the same experience, and no one could really understand exactly what is happening. I've definitely relied on the PLN connections for my own professional development.

Also, I think this is going to sound strange, but I think that being on Twitter and being part of a PLN keeps me on track. I'm conversing with some people that I consider to be very high level administrators, and without social media, I wouldn't even know that this level even existed. To know that there are people out there doing these things has really . . . it inspires me, but it also holds me accountable to my own performance in a way that I don't think existed before. I could be the best principal in my supervisory unit in my area, and if I weren't connected, I would stop growing. I would just say, "I'm the best." I wouldn't really say that out loud, but I've achieved what I know has got to be the best level I can get to.

By being connected and seeing what people are doing—putting themselves out there and doing these things—it reminds me every time that, oh, I've got some work to do to continue learning and growing.

CHAPTER 3—TWO TAKEAWAYS AND A TIP

- Takeaway #1—Develop a professional learning network through a medium you enjoy—Twitter, Voxer, Facebook, etc.
- Takeaway #2—Follow people you respect and find people they are following to grow your network because through these connections, you will begin to enhance and expand your perspectives and point of view.
- Tip—Start with a medium you enjoy, and extend the conversations beyond the 140 characters of Twitter, or post in different areas.

CHAPTER
4

Beyond Day to Day

Elementary Principal and Bammy Award Nominee Brad Gustafson embraces the mindset of connection, taking him beyond day to day and into an empowered learner. By virtue of being connected, he is able to interact with countless, caring educators across the country who are interested and available to offer support and perspective at a moment's notice. He uses Voxer on a regular basis, while commuting to and from school. This fall, he wanted to do something special for his teachers as they came back for a new year. A quick question on Voxer led to a great conversation, which eventually turned into a "red carpet" event with upbeat music, food, fun, and a crowd of cheering kids! The entire idea was hatched in less than five minutes via Voxer.

Brad has taken the idea of new media to his school as well. Weekly podcasts with students have replaced traditional principal newsletters. This has allowed him to spread the great things going on in his school via student voice, which has proven to be incredibly powerful. The students practice 21st-century skills while creating the podcasts, and they take their experiences back to their classrooms to build upon the opportunities teachers are providing as well. Brad integrates Twitter into his day by asking educators in his professional learning network for needed resources from his building. At a recent professional learning community (PLC) meeting, his group was discussing close reading, and a team requested some additional resources. He shared the request via Twitter, and within minutes, he had a very helpful blogpost, a user-friendly website, and a two close reading book titles from a trusted colleague. The tweet took less than thirty seconds to write and helped his team move forward in an area of need.

All of these things were possible because Brad took a few minutes here and there to step outside of his comfort zone by learning new tools and practices. Comfort zones are interesting. We all work so hard to get to them, but once we get there, we are really scared to step outside of the peace that they offer. They provide us with a sense of calm, but I question whether or not they help us to grow. If we spend too much time in the comfort zone, it is much harder to take risks and step outside. We completely understand it. There is rarely time where we take on a new activity and it turns into awesome right away. Take a pen and a piece of paper . . . Write your name on the paper with your nondominant hand. How are you feeling? Clearly, the more you practice the better it would get, but if we are constantly reminded that we're not good at a particular task, we are much less likely to continue doing it. Having said that, there are not too many things in the world that we could do right away. In essence, the learning always comes from outside our comfort zones.

Some people step out of their comfort zones and try something new. Joe's recent experience indicates just how far one can be pulled out of his or her comfort zone and how it can lead to an enlightening experience.

I was involved in an activity that didn't just fall a little outside my comfort zone, it resided miles away. I was asked to be part of a local fundraising effort titled Dancing with the Eau Claire Stars. Much like the long-running national dance competition, the event takes people from across this area and pairs them with a professional dance partner. The idea is to practice two dances for six weeks and throw all of that work on stage for one night. The dancing portion of the activity was difficult and well beyond my level of expertise, which was clearly a switch for me. I tend to pick activities where I feel like I can experience a relative level of success. I had no idea how I was going to have that feeling in a choreographed dance. We believe a number of our colleagues have the same feeling about their own professional growth. It was hard to dive into something that didn't provide immediate success. It is harder to dive into something and find out that it may take time away from an already busy day-to-day schedule of running a building or school district. The continuous race that we run shows no signs of stopping. We need to find a way to engage in the race, find our learning as a part of that race, and ensure that it becomes the new normal for the way we do business as leaders in schools. Here are a few hints as you begin your race. . . .

DON'T WAVER

The longer it takes you to make the decision, the less likely you are to do it. We tend to talk a lot in education. . . . We discuss and discuss and discuss and sometimes forget the most important part of decisions . . . actually making them. The decision to be a learner is an active one. We must be deliberate in the practice of getting better. We often have conversations with administrators that revolve around how busy their jobs are throughout the year. We completely agree and understand those points, but if we are to let the day-to-day operation take over and hinder the learning process for ourselves, we are not modeling what it means to be a continuous learner to our staff, students, and families. If we wait for the perfect time to jump into a new way of thinking or a new process, the tendency will be to push it off until the environment and situation are both perfect. News flash: It won't happen. There will always be things to do. There will always be a phone call to return, an email to answer, and a conversation to have with a staff member. Leading the learning means taking time for yourself to grow outside of those parameters. Make a decision, and move forward.

THE IMPACT OF PEERS

As administrators, we can lead the process of challenging staff members to grow outside their comfort zones, but when it comes down to the ownership of the process, the value of peers is incredible. The support from peers as you take a risk in your practice can be a true motivator by enhancing confidence, as evidenced by the information we shared earlier about how people learn within the context of a group. People want to be acknowledged for what they do, and that includes attempting to try something different. This has to be the culture of classrooms as well. Students will not go out on a limb if they feel that their friends are going to insult them or their teacher won't support them. I know really intelligent kids who do not participate in class because they are afraid of what their friends will say. I know kids who knock others down emotionally because it is easier than admitting that they don't understand or know the answer. I have worked with staff members who don't want to extend themselves for fear of what their colleagues would say. I am lucky to work in a place where the support for peers is really solid, but even in that space, it can be hard for people to step out of their comfort zones. As discussed earlier, we are a society that wants to learn together. Our brains want to interact. We have a desire to be around others. The learning process is difficult, and the impact that peers can have in the areas of encouragement and support can be the sparks we all need to continue on our journeys.

HAVE FUN

Find the fun. . . . The dance rehearsals were hard for me because every time I try to do something, I am constantly reminded that I am not good at it. I was so far out of my comfort zone. I felt awkward and frustrated when I couldn't get the steps right. I had really amazing teachers, Allie and Amber. They are great dancers but better people. They asked the right questions and pushed me to get better, while understanding that I was way out of my league. I felt like I accomplished more every time we rehearsed. They made this process so fun for me. We would laugh, shrug our shoulders, and make things up as we went, and at no point did I feel like I was a burden to their evenings. We had a blast. . . . And I was so glad I decided to take part in the process.

This feeling has to be a staple of what happens in schools. Kids need to feel like they are getting better and have ownership in how they grow. They need to see the connection to what they learn and how it will impact them moving forward. They need to see models of continuous learning and how it is relevant in their lives. We need to ask kids to step out of their comfort zones to maximize their learning, and you can be an incredible model if you step out of your own.

Adults need to feel like they can grow and not be stuck in a rut in their own professional development. We have been so guilty of professional development opportunities that fit schedules and the masses and don't cater to the individual needs of staff members. Staff members are told that they will be "professionally developed" from 8:00 to 3:00 on a random Tuesday in an auditorium on a topic that only applies to half of the group. Potential principals finish their certification areas and then are sent into a building without really knowing how to advance their learning, which they often choose not to do because the day-to-day operations of the building consume their time.

BREAK THE CYCLE

The cycle of teaching has a real opportunity to be improved if we are able to connect staff to areas of growth and prosperity in their field. They will be much more likely to take risks and learn if they are in an environment where that part of the job is valued. Think about the adults walking the hallways and classrooms in schools today. The majority of people in the field had relatively good experiences when they were in school. It was a place where they got their emotional and intellectual needs met. They made connections to teachers and had successes of some kind within the context of the school day. When they graduated, they started to think about what they wanted to do and one of the obvious occupations would be to re-enter a place where they found some success. These people were not in the majority when it came to their graduating class. They were either able to make connections to staff members or able to "do school" well and therefore found success in that space. So, when they enter the building as instructors, they tend to teach the way they were taught and try to make connections to students in the same way teachers before them had done. The issue is simply that if we only populate schools with teachers who had good experiences when they were in school, and if those teachers instruct exactly the way they were instructed as students, nothing will ever change. We will also miss making connections with the majority of students in that space because not everyone has had a solid school experience.

CHAPTER 4—TWO TAKEAWAYS AND A TIP

- Takeaway #1—Step out of your comfort zone. . . . Find something that scares you a little and make an effort to change practice because coming out of your comfort zone means you will learn something new! Starting a blog, creating a podcast, or joining in on a Twitter chat are great ways to develop your PLN and push your own thinking.

- Takeaway #2—COMMIT!! Once you make the decision to move forward, do it, and don't look back. You can start small. . . . But start somewhere, and then dive ahead. Create checkpoints. . . . And write them down! Put them in your calendar, and have alerts sent to you via email or notifications on your phone.

- Tip—Celebrate mini-victories as you start something new. Be proud. . . . You are pushing your own thinking. Taking time to give yourself some positive feedback will help move you forward when you think you can't do it.

The Impact of Sharing

Elementary school principal Melinda Miller was at a loss. She had a wonderful staff—they were great with kids—and the culture of her building was fantastic. She was clearly part of an environment that wanted to do what was best for students. The loss came in the idea that she didn't know if she was doing everything she could to help them grow as professionals. She had a weekly newsletter, would send out reminder e-mails, and would point people toward resources when they were presented to her.

Moving an already high-functioning school to the next level is one of the hardest things we can do as leaders. The thought that the group is already doing a number of things well can actually inhibit their growth. Moving people to better places is much easier when the culture of the school is toxic because everyone knows it's toxic, and they don't want to live in that world. Consequently, they have a vested interest to get better and move toward a more productive workplace. When you are in an environment that is productive, the ability to change hinges on how much your group can or will invest in getting better. It is much easier in this environment to look around and say, "Things are going really well, so why should we change anything?"

Melinda wanted to crowd-source the expertise of her staff, so she started a Google+ Community for her school. At first, she was the only one contributing to the community. Nothing was hurt in this process because there was no change from the past. Her e-mails and newsletters just got moved to the Google+ Community. Then, something happened. She was no longer the only one contributing information to the page. Staff members started to post articles and lessons that they felt would be helpful to the group. They were taking ownership of the process because they had an investment in getting better. The school staff now had a place to share and the momentum to learn together.

So you've read all about the power of being connected and know that there is a world out there at your fingertips that is ready to share, collaborate, and exchange. Over the last week, I have had several opportunities to engage with other educators who are relative tech novices about the power of social media—specifically, how Twitter has changed my world! Twitter has allowed me to personalize my professional development. Twitter has helped me establish connections (create a PLN—personal and professional learning community) with some incredibly dedicated, passionate, and knowledgeable educators who are willing to share, collaborate, and help stretch my thinking (See the list below for some of the people I have learned a lot from.). And Twitter has allowed me to make the walls of our school transparent to the community; we are proud of what we do, and we want to tell our own story!

After the many introductory questions and conversations, I thought I would put together a quick resource for getting started. Here we go . . .

1. Download the Twitter app on your iPhone, Droid, iPad, tablet, etc.

2. Create an account. You have to come up with a username/handle. Write down your password somewhere—this is important. This is an important step, so think about how you want to be identified on

Twitter as you develop your PLN. You can use your personal name, school name, or something that identifies your professional world. For example, my Twitter handle is @TonySinanis because I use it for professional purposes and I want people to find me easily.

3. Create a short bio and include a profile picture (no one wants to follow the "egg") so others can decide if they want to establish a connection with you. The picture is IMPORTANT because it allows for a more personalized virtual connection!

4. As a starting point, pick about ten different people to follow. Check out the list below for some awesome people you can learn from!

5. Start slow. . . . Lurk. . . . Scroll through your feed and click on links that interest you. Follow new people who are actively sharing resources that enhance your world. Search for hashtags that are related to topics of interest (i.e., #kinderchat, #edchat, #educoach, #NYedchat, #ptchat, etc.).

6. Jump into the deep end of the pool, and start sending some tweets. . . . Share resources, thoughts, and perspectives, and begin to build your PLN. . . . And your world will change!

So, go for it. . . . Enter the Twitterverse and have some fun learning and growing!

PEOPLE TO FOLLOW ON TWITTER

Jerry Blumengarten @cybraryman1	Todd Whitaker @ToddWhitaker	Matt Gomez @mattBgomez
Eric Sheninger @E_Sheninger	Nicholas Provenzano @thenerdyteacher	Steven Anderson @web20classroom
Erin Klein @KleinErin	Pernille Ripp @pernilleripp	Jessica Johnson @PrincipalJ
Carrie Jackson @jackson_carrie	Edudemic @Edudemic	Tom Whitby @tomwhitby

(Continued)

(Continued)

Joe Mazza @Joe_Mazza	Tom Murray @thomascmurray	Peter DeWitt @PeterMDeWitt
Edutopia @Edutopia	Josh Stumpenhorst @stumpteacher	John Schu @MrSchuReads
Elissa Malespina @elissamalespina	Kyle Pace @kylepace	Sandy Kendell @EdTechSandyK
Michael Berry @principalberry	George Couros @gcouros	Vicki Day @Victoria_Day
Curt Rees @CurtRees	Brad Gustafson @GustafsonBrad	Lisa Meade @LisaMeade23
Spike Cook @DrSpikeCook	Jimmy Casas @casas_jimmy	Daisy Dyer Duerr @DaisyDyerDuerr

Any and all of these people will give you a great start into becoming a connected educator. The impact the connected community has had on us is substantial. We never would have connected if not for Twitter and Edcamps. We would clearly not be writing a book together, which was consequently all done through Google Docs (another great connection tool). Both of us were relatively successful before becoming connected. We had accomplished a few things, and our schools had seen increases both academically and from a cultural perspective. Having said that, the change in our world after connecting to unbelievable educators across the world has been incredible. There have been multiple times where we had read a book or article, and instead of letting that be the end of the conversation, interacted with the author via social media. We have asked questions online to Todd Whitaker, Eric Sheninger, Jim Knight, and Arne Duncan. All responded. We have grown our circle to the point that if we have a particular question from a particular area, we no longer have to rely on Google, an outdated text, or the limited amount of people in our immediate circle who may be going through the same thing. We have the opportunity to ask and answer questions from the leaders in every area of K–12 and higher education. The access being connected has given us is astounding.

With that power comes a bit of responsibility. My wife, Andrea, is a nutrition therapist. She was an incredible elementary teacher and has brought that same level of instruction to helping adults to ensure that what goes into their bodies will help them perform to their highest levels. She is an unbelievable wife, an incredible mother, and liked by everyone she meets. Having said that, getting me to eat healthily was a monumental feat. I like what I like. I love chocolate, burgers, and essentially everything that contains gluten. When my wife started this nutrition journey, she would tell me how great she was feeling from the change in diet and the supplements that went along with it. She would discuss the increased energy, the way food was tasting, and the benefits to a longer and healthier life. I simply didn't care. There was no connection for me. I kept thinking about what I was missing out on and what I couldn't have as opposed to the positive side of healthy eating.

I think we, as connected educators, tend to do this with the unconnected community. Being connected does not automatically make you a great leader or a great teacher. It does not ensure that your students will learn. Conversely, being an unconnected educator does not make you a poor teacher. When connected educators talk about how much people are missing out on when they don't connect, the effect can be directly adverse to what we are hoping people do, and that is to connect with others to learn and grow together. Telling others that they have to be connected is akin to my parents delivering mandates that I didn't have any connection to in my youth. Having my wife tell me that eating healthy made her feel better didn't do anything for me personally. I was happy that she felt better, but just telling me that didn't make me want to adjust my lifestyle. I had to experience some success in that model by myself. It wasn't until I actually started, began to feel better about myself, and see the benefits firsthand that I was able to maintain a new lifestyle (That . . . and she took all of the bad food out of the house!).

Even within the connected-educator world, there is a sense of the "cool kids" table in the lunchroom. There is a thought that a number of followers on Twitter, Pinterest, or LinkedIn automatically certifies one as an expert in the field. Sometimes, folks, it is just that people have had accounts open for a long, long time.

The emphasis has to be on what is shared and how it connects to you as a learner. From that point, you will find those whom you connect with and build relationships where you can learn and grow together. One of the best parts about social media is that you get to set it up . . . for you. The people you follow, the pages you like, and the alerts and emails you get based on interest are all for you. Social media, in and of itself, is about connecting with people, but the responsibility always falls on you as an individual to develop circles of influence where you can give and take on our professional journey.

CHAPTER 5—TWO TAKEAWAYS AND A TIP

- **Takeaway #1**—Establish a digital presence, and make sure it reflects who you are as an educator and leader. Be consistent, and be transparent in your message.

- **Takeaway #2**—Follow some like-minded people on social media. You can choose to help reinforce some of your passions and beliefs. Also, follow some "unlike-minded" people to help push you out of your comfort zone and challenge your thinking.

- **Tip**—Social media is the most-underutilized free professional-development source on the planet. There are incredible learning opportunities for those willing to dive in.

Addressing the Gap

The gap—it is there whether we want to admit it or not. The gap exists for everyone. Every educator, in every classroom, in every school, and in every district, is impacted by the gap. The gap of knowledge, the gap of information, and the gap of experience are ones that impact all of us. As educators, we must accept the fact that our knowledge, information, and experiences are often limited by what we have taught within a certain context, and this limitation often becomes the gap. But the gap doesn't necessarily have to be a fixed place where we stop learning and growing. It is not the end. It is just the gap. And we have to access the information that will address the gap and help us enhance our craft and continue impacting our students, staff, and community in positive ways.

Award-winning Associate Principal Amber Teamann is committed to leading the learning at Watkins Elementary School in Wylie, Texas. She is truly leading the way in connecting her teachers to the world and telling the story of her school. She also leads by example when it comes to learning. Amber leverages social media to connect her colleagues to amazing educators across the country. Though she holds a vast amount of knowledge in a number of different areas, she also realizes that she doesn't know, and can't know, everything about every position in her school. If a physical education teacher is looking for a resource, Amber is not only able to help them connect with someone who has more expertise in that area, but the relationship that follows the connection for those educators is invaluable for the future. The resource is just the entry point to a conversation that can continue over time. In connecting her teachers to the outside world, she has created a forum for learning beyond school walls. It has opened the doors to all the different areas in her building. She has been able to connect people to resources in the areas of budgeting, human resources, instructional pedagogy, managing daily tasks, and being the instructional leader. All of these areas could elicit a full semester coursework in a graduate program, but because she is connected and learning on a consistent basis, she is able to grow her aptitude and that of those around her through the use of social media. It can be done in the context of her workday, it is free, and she does not need to be away from her family to take classes. Connecting with experts in the field on a regular basis is an incredible way to grow as an educational leader. Amber uses that mentality to hone her craft and has become the expert that people look to as they grow their own ability to lead their buildings and learning communities.

This is a very common perspective of leaders across the world. There is simply no way we can be experts in all areas. In trying to be everything to everyone, we believe there is a tendency to fall short of our own expectations. This has a negative impact on the building because, when we are trying to do everything for everyone, it tends to take away from the major initiatives we are tasked with as a lead learner in our buildings. When those things start getting missed because we are trying to do too much, the general feeling may be to question whether or not we can do our contracted work effectively.

Joe was hired as an elementary principal and superintendent in Fall Creek after one year as an elementary principal in that district.

Both jobs are difficult and had been contracted as two separate full-time positions in the past. The lure of the superintendency and the desire to continue the elementary school initiatives that had started in his first year made it easy for Joe to tell the school board he could do both effectively. The first year went really well. There were a few large-scale initiatives that he helped put into place that were successful. The social media presence, which he had exclusive rights to at the time, was very well received, and people liked the direction. After the second year, the school board asked Joe to reassign roles in the organization so he could concentrate on the superintendent position. He convinced the board to give him one more year in dual roles because of some major implementation pieces that were coming into the district, specifically, the elementary building remodel and a new reading series at that level. The results of that year were mixed. Though there was not any backlash in terms of his leadership role, he could tell that it was getting much too difficult to invest the necessary time in both areas to make a difference in the organization. It almost felt like a holding pattern. The elementary building remodel went fine, and the reading series was implemented. Both have been positive experiences, but the time dedicated to those particular areas clearly had an impact on the other, equally important pieces of his job. As the next year began, he was able to realign his administrative team and take on a curriculum-direction role in the organization that could have an impact on students and teachers across the K–12 range. The issue wasn't with the role or the day-to-day operations; instead, it was with the fact that Joe tried to do all of the work by himself. He didn't want to take away from the things going on in the classroom by assigning things to the teachers. He didn't want to overextend his administrative team by adding too much to their already full daily agenda. He didn't want his secretary to feel overwhelmed with a new superintendent in the building. All of these things led to Joe failing to find a balance for how he could logistically lead the organization.

There is a tendency to run on adrenaline in a leadership position, and we get into the crazy routines of the day only to look back after a certain amount of time and wonder if things were really being done well or just being done. When you have to spread yourself thin across a number of responsibilities, none of them get done with the high expectations you may have for yourself. Joe's jobs were getting done, but they weren't getting done at the level that he desired because he took too many things on at one time. Being the superintendent and adding curriculum direction to his role didn't make Joe's job any less stressful or busy; it just made it a different type of busy.

Many times, you don't have a voice in deciding you have too much on your plate. Teachers have expectations, parents have expectations, your supervisors and the board of education have expectations, and you are just trying to do the best you can in those roles so your competence isn't called into question. This is a common perspective in any role throughout the school. Everyone has days where he or she walks out of the building and wonders if he or she made a difference in the lives of teachers and kids. We are often placed in a scenario where big plans are made for growth and personal professional development only to be derailed by the day-to-day operation of the school. This is where filling the gaps and finding our blind spots can help us become active learners, even in the stress-filled day-to-day operation of a school or district.

FILLING GAPS

You can't know everything and should not be expected to in your position. Having said that, if you don't know the answer, you are certainly going to gain a great deal of momentum if you can connect someone to a person who does. Tony's background was in elementary education, but he has only specifically taught Grades 3, 4, and 5. Joe's experience led him to teaching kindergarten, second grade, fifth grade, and counseling before taking on the principal role. When he assumed the role of superintendent, he had no experience at the middle or high schools, outside of coaching at those levels. Inherently, there are gaps in your experience that you need to understand when you jump into a leadership role. Everyone knows they have gaps in his or her leadership ability, but what is done with that knowledge is the most important component. If we know that there are gaps in our experience or knowledge base and we turn into the experts on all things based on the title we have attained, we run the risk of alienating those who have been in those positions for years. In admitting that we don't know everything and subsequently leading the learning to get better in those particular areas, we are able to develop a sense that learning on the job is encouraged and expected.

We have found that the best way to fill our personal knowledge gaps is to start asking questions to the experts in our buildings. This gives them the value they need and deserve in their positions and helps us to build relationships with potential leaders in our buildings. In starting the conversations with these staff members, you can also have a profound impact on their learning. Through discussion of her or his expertise, inevitably there is a time where the staff member is looking for resources that she or he doesn't have or the answer to a question that he or she cannot find on his or her own. If we make a commitment to find resources in that area and share them with each other, we have our feet in the doors to collaborative learning opportunities. Now we have a gap that can be filled together, and this could lead to distributive leadership and increased ownership of learning as well as growth in an area where one felt a need to improve.

CULTIVATING RELATIONSHIPS

To take that concept to the next level, we should connect the in-house experts in our schools to national experts through the use of social media. This has made a profound impact in our experience. Connecting the local experts to the national experts allows staff members in our schools to begin conversations that lead to relationships that could be beneficial beyond a particular need. Someone who is connected through social media may not know the answer to a question either, but her or his network allows her or him to ask more people and get the desired resource. When our in-house staff members see the power of social media in this regard, there is an increased likelihood that they will be willing to reach out to national experts if a future need arises. The power of social media is not only that we can access experts but, at different times, we can take on the role of expert and share information that we know a lot about and support the novices within our online communities of practice.

The impact of those relationships on our staff members can be profound. We have taken the learning outside of the school walls and opened them up to an opportunity that will benefit everyone's professional development moving forward. We are much more engaged as learners if there is a personal connection to a process or person. As leaders, we have seen tremendous growth in our staff members when they are able to develop relationships with people across the world who are considered experts in their particular areas.

Let's take ourselves for examples. We have only physically been in the same space three times. However, the relationship we have cultivated through sharing resources has afforded us the opportunity to coauthor two books, host a podcast, and speak at multiple events across the country. This is what professional development looks like in the twenty-first century. We can learn, grow, and take risks with our practice because we go beyond the four walls of our context to address the gap. We are not allowing the gap to inhibit our work; in fact, we are using it as a catalyst to embrace innovation and disruption and take our learning to new levels.

DREAMS AND GOALS

There is a distinct difference between dreams and goals. Dreams happen when we are thinking about what we want our lives to look like. Dreaming about what we want life to look like often brings good feelings and ideas to mind. Goals take those dreams and thoughts and make them much more accountable; we can clearly assess if we have achieved goals as opposed to just remaining in a dream state. We dream about a ton of stuff!!! Green Bay

Packer Super Bowl victories, a school environment where everyone feels happy and productive, a world where kids get all of their needs met on a regular basis, a full head of hair (and enough hair product to style it), or providing for our families. Goals take those thoughts and help provide focus and road maps for us to accomplish things we have set out to do. We need to take the thoughts that make us so happy right before we fall asleep and put them into action so we can smile when we are awake.

The challenge for leaders is that we try to get better at too many things and subsequently get better at none. We discuss how we can improve in an area but rarely find the time to dig deep and get better in our leadership practice. We read books and think of ways to implement those ideas, and then the day-to-day operations take over, and our growth timelines get pushed back.

Every year, Joe asks his staff to come with "My Three." They find three things that they can complete in one day and, when accomplished, walk out feeling good about what happened. There will be days that they struggle to meet the three goals and other days that they will have them met by the time kids arrive. . . . But it is a constant reminder that little victories can bring big successes. Joe has his staff post their three by their desks as a constant reminder that there are certain things that need attention for us to feel self-worth in what we do. With this reminder, we are more likely to focus in times where we are not feeling our best. This concept can be used to drive our own learning. Having a "My Three" designated for our personal professional growth can help us as administrators focus on resources to improve while we are locked into the daily grind of running a building and creating the best space possible for kids. Tweeting an article, having a conversation with a staff member, connecting to people, taking part in a chat on Twitter, finding one resource to help a colleague, or reading a few pages of a book can all be used in our "My Three" to drive our own learning. Remember, goals are for us—for us to grow, enhance our craft, and address the gap. When Joe asks his staff to develop their three, they do not have to be turned in, graded, or revamped for grammatical errors. They are unequivocally theirs. The only thing he asks is that they help the staff member grow as a professional and positively impact kids—no judgment at all. As leaders, we have to accept that people all come into the job at different levels, and their learning baselines start at different places. To tell someone that the three he or she focused on are not rigorous enough or are not meaningful to you takes away from his or her value as a learner. We have to trust our staff and meet them where they are, not where we are on the learning continuum.

CHAPTER 6—TWO TAKEAWAYS AND A TIP

- **Takeaway #1**—Figure out what your gaps are, professionally speaking, and try to address them through any social media platform that is comfortable to you. Remember, you don't have to be an expert on everything; you just have to be able to find the experts to get the information you need.

- **Takeaway #2**—Remember that we need to take the thoughts that make us so happy right before we fall asleep and put them into action so we can smile when we are awake and at school with our staff and kids. We must turn our dreams into achievable goals.

- **Tip**—Start everyday by establishing your "My Three" for the day, and make your goal accomplishing those three things each day.

CHAPTER

7

Getting the Most Out of Social Media Tools

The idea of time comes up often when we talk about being a continuous learner. Many people connect learning to their workday. Being a continuous learner doesn't mean you have to be plugged in all day, every day. Having said that, we have found that connecting your personal and professional platforms can be helpful to your learning. We check Twitter on a regular basis. This time is often spent reviewing things that are going on in the education world but also connecting on a personal level with people we have built relationships with over time. It has turned into a balance of learning and relaxation. For us, personal professional development and our own social media footprint melded together. We live virtually in places that we utilize for professional development. Consequently, it has made learning a much easier task in the long run. Though we would never advocate being plugged in all the time, we do feel that connecting the platforms allows you the flexibility to learn and connect socially from the same place. Having personal and professional accounts for your learning might inhibit the ease of sharing or connecting, which could lead to a lack of interest. The logistics of the process have a substantial impact on the willingness to dive into the process. If navigating social media is too hard or cumbersome, it is very easy to feel like it is piling onto an already full plate. Here are some platforms that align well with being connected:

TWITTER

Twitter is our first stop for professional development. As you have probably noticed in the themes throughout the book, this is the medium we feel most comfortable with to grow our knowledge and expand our circles professionally. Twitter allows you the opportunity to find areas of interest, connect with great educators, and flatten the walls of your school to provide a rich environment for all staff and students.

How to Use Twitter for Professional and Personal Development

- Participate in chats to exchange ideas, resources, and techniques. There are an abundance of chats. See the companion website for a comprehensive list of regularly scheduled chats.

- Develop and nurture your personal/professional learning network through the connections you establish on Twitter. The members of your PLN become your go-to people when you have a question, issue, or challenge; the flow of ideas can be incredibly powerful.

- Focus on one thing at a time and find the right people and hashtags to access the most relevant and useful information in that area. For example, if you are considering a 1:1 iPad implementation, connect with others who have done this, and find hashtags that deal with the topic.

FACEBOOK

Facebook continues to be the monster of all social media sites. Though it may be replaced with something else in the future, it needs to be utilized for communication. The site has 128 million daily users in the United States of America, which indicates that Facebook still has the largest reach in the social media world (Smith, 2014).

Initially, we used Facebook as a tool to connect with family and friends. As we have built relationships with educators across the world, we have found the lines blurred between checking status updates from friends and items professional educators are sharing in that space. We often will scroll through our pages and find things that would help us in our job as well as add deposits to our emotional bank accounts. As Facebook fan pages have moved from teams to educational organizations and groups, we have found that adding those to the stream has been helpful as well.

How to Use Facebook for Professional and Personal Development

- Like pages of groups, schools, and organizations from around the globe that can help expand your network of ideas.
- Post questions, needs, and ideas across multiple platforms, including Facebook, to get responses from people in the form of links, videos, and posts.
- Share all the amazing things (and even the challenges) unfolding in your school as a way to elevate the level of transparency and potentially connect with other learning communities in similar situations!

GOOGLE+ COMMUNITIES

Google+ Communities continue to gain momentum in the educational world. We have found this to be a great place to share ideas and connect with educators on a professional basis. The premise behind Google+ Communities is to be an open place to share information and connections. The idea that many people already have a Gmail account helps drive participation. Communities can be closed; so you can create your own for faculty, a regional or state group, or just a collection of educators across the world who you would want to share with on a regular basis. Most communities in the education world that we have experienced are open to all. EdTech, PLCs, and School Leadership have all been very popular since the inception of Google+ Communities in 2012. It is a great place to learn and grow.

How to Use Google+ for Professional and Personal Development

- Create a community for your school staff so they can share ideas and resources to enhance practice within your school (see Melinda Miller's vignette in Chapter 5).

- Join existing communities made up of other educators as a platform to share resources, ideas, and situations. Circles of educators give one access to relevant blogposts, videos, and other materials that could easily impact practice within your own school, which was recently done by the group implementing the School Administrator Virtual Mentoring Program (#SAVMP).

- Create a community for your own school community (including both students and families) as a space to maintain an ongoing dialogue and spotlight all the amazing things happening in your space.

VOXER

Voxer has been an absolute game changer for our personal professional development. Voxer is a messaging app that allows people to have asynchronous discussions regarding a particular topic. It is essentially taking a Twitter chat to a new level and allowing your voice to be heard. Voxer groups can be set up with colleagues in your area or people across the world. Voxer allows you to record your voice, text, or a link to an outside source. Twitter chats have now taken to Voxer to get beyond the 140 characters allowed in that space and bring about a whole new level of engagement.

CHAPTER 7—TWO TAKEAWAYS AND A TIP

- **Takeaway #1**—Find professional development in a place where you already live from a social media perspective. Whether it is Twitter, Voxer, or a Google+ Community, the platform supports this idea of social interactions that lead to sharing, learning, and enhancing one's craft.

- **Takeaway #2**—Start in an area where you feel comfortable and dip your toe into new media when ready. . . . But don't wait long. . . . Start something now because your learning must be your priority!

- **Tip**—The list of possible social media tools to increase your professional experience continues to grow. Don't let that throw you; it is about the process and not the tool.

IT'S A WRAP!

Digital tools of today will be replaced with newer, faster, and more productive tools in the future. The gold is not in the tool but the process. As leaders, we have an obligation to seek out and model opportunities that could help our students, staff, and community. We need to provide resources and time for people to dive into the process and grow through ownership of learning. Self-guided exploration of learning is great for both students and staff. We don't need to have all the answers and often won't, but if we are seen as leading the learning, we will be in a better place. People are often placed into leadership positions because of a great interview or because they had experienced some success in a different role. If we want to lead learning organizations, then let's lead the learning in that organization! If continuous learning becomes the new normal for you as a leader in your school, district, or community, the impact can be dramatic.

Take the first step. . . . Connect with someone on Twitter, join a Google+ Community, or set up an account on Flipboard to deliver personalized learning to a device. Whatever you do, just start. You will be able to provide more opportunities for staff, students will see you modeling the learning, and the community will know that you value growth in not only staff and students but yourself as well.

References

Alderton, E., Brunsell, E., & Bariexca, D. (2011). The end of isolation. *Journal of Online Learning and Teaching, 7*(3), 1–16.

Barnes, C. A., Camburn, E., Sanders, B. R., & Sebastian, J. (2010). Developing instructional leaders: Using mixed methods to explore the black box of planned change in principals' professional practice. *Educational Administration Quarterly, 46*(2), 241–279.

Boerema, A. J. (2011). Challenging and supporting new leader development. *Educational Management Administration & Leadership, 39*(5), 554–567.

Boyatzis, R. E., & McKee, A. (2005). *Resonant leadership: Renewing yourself and connecting with others through mindfulness, hope, and compassion.* Boston, MA: Harvard Business Press.

Brennan, W. V. (2013). *School principals and virtual learning: A catalyst to personal and organizational learning* (Doctoral dissertation). Retrieved from http://fordham.bepress.com/dissertations/AAI3551332/

Brown, K. M., Anfara, V. A., Hartman, K. J., Mahar, R. J., & Mills, R. (2002). Professional development of middle level principals: Pushing the reform forward. *Leadership and Policy in Schools 1*(2), 107–143.

Caldwell, S. D. (1986). Effective practices for principals' inservice. *Theory into Practice, 25*(3), 174–178.

Cochran-Smith, M. & Lytle, S. L. (2009). *Inquiry as stance: Practitioner research for the next generation.* New York, NY: Teachers College Press.

Elias, S. (2012). *Implications of online social network sites on the personal and professional learning of educational leaders* (Doctoral dissertation). Retrieved from http://digitool.library.colostate.edu/R/?func=dbin -jump-full&object_id=170454&local_base=GEN01

Elmore, R., & Burney, D. (1999). Investing in teacher learning: Staff development and instructional improvement. In Darling-Hammond, L. & Sykes, G. (Eds.), *Teaching as the learning profession: Handbook of policy and practice* (pp. 236–291). San Francisco, CA: Jossey-Bass.

Engels, N., Hotton, G., Devos, G., Bouckenooghe, D., & Aelterman, A. (2008). Principals in schools with a positive school culture. *Educational Studies, 34*(3), 159–174. doi: 10.1080/03055690701811263

Fullan, M. (2009). Leadership development: The larger context. *Educational Leadership, 67*(2), 45–49.

Galagan, P. (2009). Twitter as a learning tool. Really. *T + D, 63*(3), 28–29, 31.

Gerard, L. F., Bowyer, J. B., & Linn, M. C. (2008). Principal leadership for technology-enhanced learning in science. *Journal of Science Education and Technology, 17*(1), 1–18.

Greenhow, C. (2009). Tapping the wealth of social networks for professional development. *Learning & Leading With Technology, 36*(8), 10–11.

Grissom, J. A., & Harrington, J. R. (2010). Investing in administrator efficacy: An examination of professional development as a tool for enhancing principal effectiveness. *American Journal of Education, 116*(4), 583–612.

Hallinger, P. (1992). The evolving role of American principals: From managerial to instructional to transformational leaders. *Journal of Educational Administration, 30*(3), 35–48.

Hallinger, P. (2003). Leading educational change: Reflections on the practice of instructional and transformational leadership. *Cambridge Journal of Education, 33*(3), 329–351.

Johnson, N. (1994). Education reforms and professional development of principals: Implications for universities. *Journal of Educational Administration, 32*(2), 5–20.

Lave, J., & Wenger, E. (1991). *Situated learning: Legitimate peripheral participation.* New York, NY: Cambridge University Press.

Leithwood, K., & Jantzi, D. (2000). The effects of transformational leadership on organizational conditions and student engagement with school. *Journal of Educational Administration, 38*(2), 112–129.

Lytle, J. H. (2010). *Working for kids: Educational leadership as inquiry and invention.* Lanham, MD: Rowmann & Littlefield.

Ondrejka, C. (2008). Education unleashed: Participatory culture, education, and innovation in Second Life. In K. Salen (Ed.), *The ecology of games: Connecting youth, games, and learning* (pp. 229–252). Cambridge, MA: MIT Press.

Perez, L. (2012). Innovative professional development: Expanding your professional learning network. *Knowledge Quest, 40*(3), 20–22.

Reardon, R. M. (2011). Elementary school principals' learning-centered leadership and educational outcomes: Implications for principals' professional development. *Leadership and Policy in Schools, 10*(1), 63–83.

Smith, C. (2014, December 17). By the numbers: 200+ amazing Facebook user & demographic statistics [Weblog post]. Retrieved from http://expandedramblings.com/index.php/by-the-numbers-17-amazing-facebook-stats/#.UxtqEuddWrc

Spanneut, G., Tobin, J., & Ayers, S. (2012). Identifying the professional development needs of public school principals based on the interstate school leader licensure consortium standards. *NASSP Bulletin, 96*(1), 67–88.

Supovitz, J., Sirinides, P., & May, H. (2010). How principals and peers influence teaching and learning. *Educational Administration Quarterly, 46*(1), 31–56.

Waters, J. T., Marzano, R. J., & McNulty, B. A. (2003). *Balanced leadership: What 30 years of research tells us about the effect of leadership on student achievement.* Aurora, CO: Mid-continent Research for Education and Learning.

Wenger, E. (1998). *Communities of practice: Learning, meaning, and identity.* New York, NY: Cambridge University Press.

Wenger, E. (2000). Communities of practice and social learning systems. *Organization, 7*(2), 225–246.

CORWIN
A SAGE Company

Corwin is committed to improving education for all learners by publishing books and other professional development resources for those serving the field of PreK–12 education. By providing practical, hands-on materials, Corwin continues to carry out the promise of its motto: **"Helping Educators Do Their Work Better."**